# A CHURCH NEAR YOU

*An introduction to Anglican churches from Cumbria to Cornwall*

*written and illustrated by*
# DENIS DUNSTONE

*with a Foreword by* SIMON JENKINS

UMBRIA PRESS

Copyright © Denis Dunstone 2023

Denis Dunstone has asserted his right under the Copyright, Designs and Patents Act 1988 to be identified as the author of this work.

First published in 2023 by Umbria Press

Umbria Press
2 Umbria Street
London SW15 5DP
www.umbriapress.co.uk

Designed and typeset in Minion
by Louise Millar

Printed by Bell & Bain Ltd, Glasgow
bell-bain.com

ISBN 978-1-910074-45-9

## Contents

| | | |
|---|---|---|
| **Foreword** | | 4 |
| National Churches Trust and Churches Conservation Trust | | 6 |
| **Introduction** | | 7 |
| Chapter 1 | **Beginnings** | 9 |
| Chapter 2 | **Towers** | 49 |
| Chapter 3 | **Layouts** | 101 |
| Chapter 4 | **Enhancement** | 119 |
| Chapter 5 | **Doorways** | 147 |
| Chapter 6 | **Casualties** | 173 |
| **Index** – Locations listed by county | | 204 |

Chedworth in Gloucestershire, deep in the country.

# Foreword by **Simon Jenkins**

A parish church embodies communal England. It is cherished by all, by worshippers and non-worshippers alike. All would feel a sense of loss were churches to go the way of medieval castles and become empty ruins. Whenever I ask people about their local church, I find most say simply, 'Oh it's not for me.' They still admit they would miss it if it were not there. As Betjeman wrote, 'It's strange that those we miss the most/ Are those we took for granted.'

As the number of unused churches rises into the thousands, their future guardianship has become a national challenge. It is therefore vital to spread an understanding of their past to guide possible new purposes for their future. Crucial is to see these buildings as they once were and must be again, representative of their wider communities. They were creations of a collective faith and craftsmanship on the part of what was once an entire parish. They remain temples of local history, ceremony, pride and congregation. They can and must continue to perform that function.

Few Britons today are familiar with ecclesiastical liturgy and its presentation in architecture. Few know the bible characters portrayed on a church's exterior or the significance of chancels, towers, aisles, gables and buttresses. That is why they should be shown the language of medieval churches, if only to appreciate the one quality they share in common, that of a serene beauty. People should appreciate the style of their region, the stone of their neighbourhood, the handiwork of citizens past and the meaning of the memorials they fashioned. Children should be taught these things in school. Churches need bringing to life.

To this end Denis Dunstone has performed a signal service. He has described churches clearly and in lay terms. He has rightly concentrated on exteriors, for they are what local people see, often many times a day. Through his eyes, we see the extraordinary variety of English churches down the ages. To him they are not, as many can seem, austere edifices bathed in silent shadows. They are rich evocations of the past. His towers are beckoning, his porches inviting, his stones coated in sun and colour. All convey his personal delight. They are truly treasures.

Only when we speak Dunstone's language of churches will these buildings come to be restored and reinvigorated for the towns and villages that created them many centuries ago. They must be public spaces, personal as well as collective as they have been through most of English history. Only then will they be truly safe.

St Edmund Church, Southwold, Suffolk

## NATIONAL CHURCHES TRUST

The National Churches Trust helps to keep the UK's chapels and meeting houses open in in use.

Churches are impressive, exciting and surprising places. Whether seeking quiet reflection, access to critical community services, a warm welcome, a place to worship, or a space to explore, we believe they should be loved and supported. Available to all. Working together with churches of all denominations cross all four nations, we help to maintain these wonderful historic buildings and keep them thriving today, and tomorrow.

Our charity has a fascinating history that begins at the start of the 19th century with the Incorporated Church Building Society, founded in 1818 to enlarge and build new churches. In 1953 the Historic Churches Preservation Trust assumed responsibility for the society's affairs with a new focus on helping parish churches in a poor state of repair.

The National Churches Trust was created in 2007 to carry on the work of the Historic Churches Preservation Trust (HCPT), which was set up in 1953. Since then we have helped over 2,000 churches with funding for urgent repairs. Our mission is to support and celebrate churches, provide advice and information, and to speak up for churches of all Christian denominations and the work they do. Our supporters include Sir Michael Palin, Huw Edwards and Bill Bryson. We were honoured that HM Queen Elizabeth was our Patron throughout her reign.

If you love churches, you can support our work and help more churches stay open by becoming a Friend. Find out more at nationalchurchestrust.org

## CHURCHES CONSERVATION TRUST

The Churches Conservation Trust is the national charity saving historic churches at risk. The charity looks after over 350 historic churches around England. The Trust was born in 1968 by an act of the Church of England, approved by Parliament, entitled The Pastoral Measure: Ecclesiastical law.

Under this law, churches of exceptional historic, architectural, or archaeological significance that would otherwise be forced to close are vested to the Trust. The Trust cares for them, carries out much needed conservation work, and explores appropriate, community-based new uses.

Although CCT churches do not have a congregation or a vicar, they remain consecrated. Some are still used for church services on special occasions or on specific days during the year.

These churches are kept open and accessible to the public, and in total, they welcome over 1.9 million people each year. All churches in the Trust's care are listed buildings, with many of them Grade I listed, and a few listed as Scheduled Ancient Monuments.

With our help and your vital support, we can ensure the long-term sustainability of these unique and special spaces that would otherwise be forgotten without communities to love and care for them. Learn more about our work and how you can help on our website, visitchurches.org.uk.

# Introduction

This book is an introduction to old churches. It is deliberately unsophisticated; the author is not an architect. It is hoped that it will arouse interest in the subject by concentrating on the more obvious characteristics, and serve as a way of broadening interest in the amazing heritage we have in this country. Most of the churches covered are in England, though Monmouthshire is included for the interest and relevance of its churches.

The foundation of this book lies in 19 studies made by county. This book picks the most interesting and those which have sometimes surprising similarities and contrasts. It covers only Anglican churches, and only those built before 1700. It focusses on the exterior, as this is where the history of a building is most clearly revealed. This is at the price of excluding wonderful internal features such as paintings, monuments and elaborate roofs.

Many of these buildings are at risk, partly due to declining congregations, and while in the end it is local people who have to look after their treasures, there are supporting organisations such as the **National Churches Trust (NCT)**, the **Churches Conservation Trust (CCT)**, the **Friends of Friendless Churches**, and the **County Trusts** who raise money to assist. The **CCT** manages churches which have been declared unaffordable by a diocese. This book is sold in support of the NCT and CCT.

The church at Bosham, on the edge of Chichester Harbour in West Sussex, is thought to be the oldest church in the county. Parts of the tower and nave are Saxon and it features in the Bayeux Tapestry.

## Chapter 1: **Beginnings**

In England early churches were built of wood. Only one survives, not far from London at Greensted in Essex. The development of masonry churches from about 600 was influenced by the Celtic church, from Ireland, Scotland and the north of England. From the European continent came another stream of Christian teaching in the footsteps of St Augustine. While the Celtic favoured a church consisting of nave and a square ended chancel, with later a tower at the west end of the nave, the Continental favoured a central tower, sometimes functioning as a nave, and a rounded chamber at the east and west ends called an apse. Only one original west end apse survives in England, at Langford, also in Essex. They are however frequently found in Germany and one was built in the 18th century in Monmouthshire, not far from Abergavenny. This was on a private estate church belonging to a Catholic family and was disguised as an orangery. Another was built in the 19th century on a church in Chatham which is now redundant.

The east apse has survived at a few churches across England, but most fell victim to the extension of chancels which occurred widely after about 1200.

In the period before the Norman Conquest the Anglo Saxon church had a number of distinctive characteristics. Some of these continued after the Conquest, when the Normans instituted a major church building programme.

The earliest surviving wooden church in the world is claimed to be in Essex at Greensted, near Ongar. A Celtic pattern church, the tower and dormer windows are later additions.

In the same county at Bradwell near the Thames Estuary is a Celtic church built in about 680, founded by Christians from the north of England.

BEGINNINGS

The church at Newhaven in Sussex has an Anglo Saxon tower and an apse adjoining it. It was built in the Norman period, but the Saxon masons carried on with what was familiar to them. It was typically Saxon style to place the tower next to the chancel, whether or not it was in the form of an apse.

Probably the oldest church in Lincoln, St Mary le Wigford with its Saxon tower now finds itself adjacent to the railway.

No Anglo Saxon churches survive intact, but there are several nearly complete examples and a few towers scattered across the country from Northumberland to Gloucestershire. They are characterised by quoins (corners) with what is termed 'long and short work'; that is alternating slabs laid to give rigidity to the quoin. They also have pilasters or lesnes, stone strips which have the appearance of timber, which may have been the intention. Another distinctive feature is the bell opening in the form of a double arch supported by a single column.

St Benet's in Cambridge has the Anglo Saxon bell opening

Barton on Humber in Lincolnshire has all these features.

BEGINNINGS

Earls Barton in Northamptonshire has an exceptionally elaborate tower with lesnes and 'long and short work' on the quoins.

Earls Barton                    Bywell

Bywell in Northumberland at a crossing of the Tyne is an earlier pre-conquest Saxon church with its original Saxon tower at the west end of the nave, in Celtic style.

Brixworth in Northamptonshire, founded in about 680, is the oldest large church surviving in Northern Europe.

In this drawing the firm line represents Brixworth today and the dotted line the original. It would have had a central tower, an apse, at the west end of the nave a narthex (like a lobby) and along the nave small chambers called porticus which led later to the porch.

Two city centre Saxon towers similar in appearance are
St Michael in Oxford and All Saints Colchester

St Michael, Oxford                All Saints Colchester

Both reveal the characteristic stone work on the quoins,
though the bell opening is more typical at Oxford. Both have
later church naves. Colchester has noticeably more brick work,
probably due to the availability of Roman bricks

Another ancient church is at Deerhurst in Gloucestershire. The nave and apse were built in the 8th century and the tower was added on a west porch in the 10th century. It also had porticos on each side of the nave as at Brixworth.
The aisles are later.

BEGINNINGS

At Monkwearmouth in County Durham, a tall Saxon west tower was built in the 10th century on a 7th century porch. The nave of the church is also Saxon but with later windows

# A CHURCH NEAR YOU

At Clapham in Bedfordshire there is a Saxon tower, 87 ft. tall. Some consider it the finest of all the survivors.

Clapham

Sompting

The Saxon tower at Sompting in Sussex has an unusual Germanic top above the typical bell openings.

Wickham in Berkshire has double bell openings.

Wickham

The most complete and unaltered Saxon church in England is at Bradford on Avon in Wiltshire. It has the Saxon characteristics, is tall and narrow with small windows, but is elaborately decorated with blind arches and pilasters. The porticus on the north side has a typically narrow Saxon door.

It is in occasional use but is subsidiary to the later church in the distance.

Great Dunham in Norfolk, near Swaffham, has a near perfect Saxon so-called axial church, with central tower, Saxon bell openings and quoins.

St John, Duxford in South Cambridgeshire has a seriously buttressed tower and a north aisle resulting in a gallery of arches within.

Coln St Denis in Gloucestershire has an addition on top of the tower but is otherwise unaltered. The north side shows signs of damp.

The oldest building in the borough of Slough, Berkshire, is St Laurence Upton cum Chalvey. On the north side it is a nearly perfectly preserved early axial church.

Oxfordshire has two contrasting axial churches. Iffley near Oxford is a nearly perfect Norman construction with a few later windows, while Cassington, also near the city, is more altered.

The church at Shipley, Sussex, near the Knepp Estate, is little altered. The chancel has survived the 13th century trend to lengthen them.

On the other hand Etchingham in Kent has a north aisle and a tower turret. This contained a stairway for access to the belfry. In Kent central towers are found mainly east of a line from Faversham to Folkestone.

Bedford has three central towered churches, more than any other town in England. St Mary's is an axial church in the care of the CCT.

Stewkley in Buckinghamshire is a virtually pure axial relic.

The axial church at South Lopham in Norfolk has fine Norman blind arcading on the tower.

St Mary de Lode in Gloucester is a good example of the axial Saxon church developed and perpetuated by the Normans.

The simplicity of the nave, tower, chancel layout was elaborated over time, but at Hewelsfield near the Welsh border in Gloucestershire the change has been minor, and less than at St Mary's where a north aisle has been added.

At Burnham Overy on the Norfolk coast the church was originally without transepts, but there is some evidence that these were added and later taken away. There remains a long south aisle.

At Pirton in Hertfordshire the transepts have disappeared giving the church the appearance of an axial church, which was its original form.

The presence of central towers is mainly in the southern part of England as far north as Yorkshire. Monmouthshire in Wales has a high proportion, possibly due to a strong Norman presence. At Magor in Monmouthshire there is a parvise over the north porch.

The influence spread to Somerset at Clevedon on the Bristol Channel. Here a cruciform format was achieved by adding two transepts.

The cruciform layout spread across the country. At Filey on the Yorkshire coast there is evidence of an earlier higher nave and transept.

At East Garston in the west of Berkshire there is a good cruciform example with a later south aisle with battlements. These were a decorative feature popular from about 1300 and had no military function.

At Bromyard in Herefordshire there is a cruciform church with central tower.

Amesbury in Wiltshire is one of a string of minster churches spreading from Northamptonshire to Somerset.

# BEGINNNGS

Two central towers in close proximity to one another are at Portchester at the end of Portsmouth Harbour and Havant. The former has a simple undeveloped plan; Havant has had more additions.

The church beside the Roman lighthouse at Dover was originally axial but transepts were added to make it cruciform.

Stow in Lindsey in Lincolnshire is an almost perfect cruciform church, little altered over the centuries.

St Cross at Winchester is also cruciform as built.

BEGINNNGS

Waithe in Lincolnshire is an early Norman version with an apse. The Normans developed the cruciform church which continued to receive alterations, in some cases changing the character completely. However the broach spire sits happily on the Norman tower of cruciform East Meon in Hampshire.

After the Conquest the Normans embarked on a programme of church building. Some were developed from the Saxon style, cruciform with a central tower; others had a west tower from the start.

A fine example exists at St Margaret-at-Cliffe. This is a small village near Dover in Kent, better known for its bay. The church has a massive Norman tower, blind arcading, a south aisle and a west door with a porch. It has been little altered.

It has an even more splendid rival at St Peter in Northampton.

This church with its extensive blind arcading and colourful tower is managed by the CCT.

It is an example of a resourceful approach to preserving a redundant church, whereby a local pub, that had been closed, has been acquired to be run as a supporting visitor experience.

Tewkesbury Abbey, in Gloucestershire, now the Parish Church, is a fine Norman building. The tower has the elaborate blind arcading seen at Sandwich, East Meon and Devizes.

# BEGINNNGS

The Normans were skilled at decorating stone walls with arches and adaptations of arches. This blind arcading was highly developed and at Castle Rising near Kings Lynn in Norfolk the west end of the cruciform church is a feast.

The same decoration was provided on the tower of the cruciform church at Sandwich in Kent

Norman decoration on a transept at Christchurch Abbey in Hampshire.

Dunstable Abbey, now the parish church, in Bedfordshire has a west front which is a supreme fantasy of blind arches, with a massive Norman doorway, but 'pointed Gothic' in the blind arcading. In the same county Felmersham has a more restrained display on the west front.

Some early Norman Celtic churches were elaborately decorated, none more than Barfrestone in Kent with its typically Norman blind arcading. Kilpeck in Herefordshire is more restrained, but a gem.

Kempley in the Forest of Dean is a good example of the basic Celtic church with a later west tower. It is notable for its wall paintings, the oldest in England, and is unusual in being managed by English Heritage. The tower has a good example of a pyramid roof, this one extending outside the walls of the tower. In the same county Duntisbourne Rouse is built on a steep slope and has an unusual crypt under the chancel. The tower has a so called saddleback roof.

The only original west apse left in England is at Langford in Essex. The church steeple is in an unusual location, north of the chancel. At Pentlow in Essex near the Suffolk border there is an east apse on a church with a round tower.

Three apsed churches: Checkendon in Oxfordshire, Wissington in Suffolk and East Ham in London, formerly Essex.

At Madley in Herefordshire the apse is polygonal and has a crypt.

Bluntisham in Cambridgeshire has another variation on the apse. It would be interesting to know how this came about in a quiet corner of the fens.

Three apses survive in Yorkshire. At Birkin near Ferrybridge there is a perfectly preserved example complete with Saxon pilasters.

At Sutton near Dover there is another example with similar appearance.

At Portskewett in Monmouthshire, the Severn ferry point, the Norman Celtic church is a near perfect survivor.

Worth in Kent is a Saxon church with a 19th century tower. The apse is decorated with Saxon pilasters.

At Lastingham in Yorkshire there is a Saxon apse with crypt below, as at Madley in Herefordshire.

At Wing in Buckinghamshire there is a fine Saxon apse on a nave which, apart from later windows, has a Saxon aisle and arcade.

# Chapter 2: **Towers**

Churches have had towers from the early days. It may have been no more than a bell-cote, but something was needed to hold a bell. The role of the bell was as a summons, but also in some cases as an alarm. Towers developed with masonry churches in the Anglo Saxon period. They had a number of roles. In areas of conflict they were a refuge or even a fortress; near the coast they served as an aid to navigation; up the east side of England they were a way marker; in York, illuminated, they served as a guide. Later they became a matter of rivalry between towns, and between landowners.

Initially they were capped with a pyramid-shape roof, but this slowly grew and by the 13th century spires were emerging. Here there was serious rivalry. Ulm in Germany has a steeple (tower and spire combined) over 500 ft. tall. Salisbury Cathedral has the tallest in England at 404 ft.

The style of English towers has varied over the centuries; Anglo Saxon were tall and narrow, Norman were stout and massive, as though built with defence in mind. They gradually became more elegant with false battlements and pinnacles. Then after 1350 they became taller and more elaborate, especially in Somerset. There is no satisfactory explanation for the magnificence and sophistication of Somerset church towers. They are rivalled in Suffolk and Gloucestershire, while in Northamptonshire the existence of good quality masonry enabled soaring spires, but the number in Somerset gives them an important place in the documentation of English art.

The tower at Stoke-by-Nayland church in Suffolk has fine proportions, modest decoration and an ability to fit gently into its site. For many it is the perfection of English style.

# TOWERS

In Cambridgeshire the largest church is at Mildenhall. This is a county with a range of styles, from the tall masonry spires of Huntingdon to the shorter spires in the south.

The tower at New Romney in Kent is a fine Norman edifice built to make an impact in what was then an important port. As a result of earth movement the west door is now below road level.

The tower at Milton Regis near Sittingbourne in north Kent is large and robust. The church has Roman material and the north wall is partly a Roman wall from the 4th century.

One of the features of medieval towers was the external turret containing the stairs for access to the belfry. In some counties these are a feature of the design; in others they are tucked away as though an embarrassment. At Beaconsfield in Buckinghamshire the turret is made a feature…

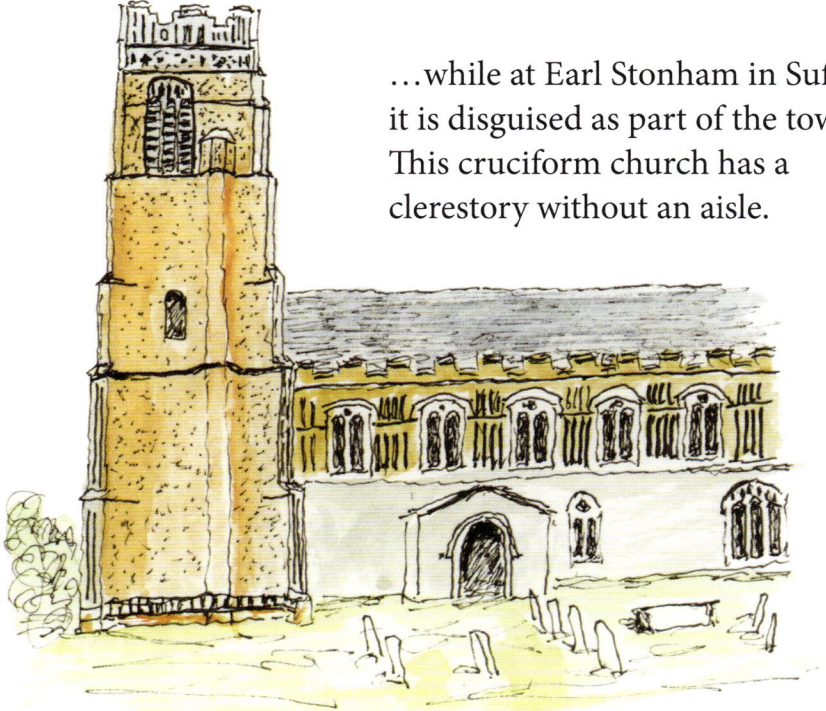

…while at Earl Stonham in Suffolk it is disguised as part of the tower. This cruciform church has a clerestory without an aisle.

# A CHURCH NEAR YOU

At Cavendish in Suffolk the turret is a feature and has a bell on top.

# TOWERS

The church at Meare in Somerset has a large turret while Tintinhull in the same county is more modest. Edington in Wiltshire has three turrets, one for the parvise, one on the tower for the belfry and another on the transept to gain access to the tower turret, by creeping along inside the transept.

Yorkshire is not a county of high towers. Tickhill near Doncaster is one of the higher at 124 ft.

If height is a criterion of excellence, Lincolnshire takes the prize. At 282 ft. Louth is the tallest church in England, closely followed by Grantham at 272 ft.

Louth                                   Grantham

Boston in Lincolnshire, without a spire has the highest tower in England at 266 ft. and has a splendid octagonal lantern.

The octagon was a popular style possibly influenced by the lantern at Ely Cathedral. At Swaffham Prior, also in Cambridgeshire, there are two in the same churchyard.

The church at Pontefract in Yorkshire, has an octagonal top to the central tower. Damaged in the Civil War, a smaller church was built inside the original, which is roofless.

A CHURCH NEAR YOU

Oxfordshire has an octagonal tower on the splendid cruciform church at Uffington. Near the White Horse on the Berkshire Downs, Uffington is where John Betjeman, poet laureate and lover of old churches, lived.

Wickham Market in Suffolk has an octagonal south tower with an elegant spire.

Northamptonshire is particularly strong on the octagon. The lanterns at Lowick and at Fotheringhay, and on the nave of the round church in Northampton provide variety.

# A CHURCH NEAR YOU

At Coxwold near Thirsk in Yorkshire there is a tall octagonal tower.

Doulting Church in Somerset has an octagonal central tower and a very fine porch with parvise.

TOWERS

Bloxham has the tallest spire in Oxfordshire at 198 ft. It has an elegant transition from octagonal to four sided.

Wilby in Northamptonshire also has a smooth transition.

The octagon had appeal across the country. Another in Somerset is at Barton St David, south east of Glastonbury.

St Mary's, Beverley, Yorkshire, has octagonal towers at the west end which served as lanterns to light the way to the town.

The octagonal top at Minchinhampton in Gloucestershire is rather ponderous, while the whole tower at Hockley in Essex is more balanced, in spite of the buttresses.

Kettlestone in Norfolk is rather plain, with stairway tucked into a corner.

Sutton in the Isle in Cambridgeshire has a particularly attractive octagonal lantern.

There are three octagonal naves in England, at Teignmouth in Devon, Stoney Middleton in Derbyshire and Micheldever in Hampshire. All were built in the 19th century. There was another at Wisbech, but it was demolished in 1952.

# TOWERS

Somerset is unique in the number and quality of its late medieval towers. Appropriately one of the finest is at Taunton. There is a massive version as a central tower at Ilminster.

Some of the oldest towers are so-called round towers. Out of 185 in England, Norfolk has 124. It is thought that the reason for their construction was that in areas with little masonry available, the round tower avoided the problem of building firm quoins (corners) with flint or rubble.

One of the oldest is East Lexham, near Swaffham, in Norfolk.

There are three in Sussex, all in or near Lewes. Southease has an unusual hipped chancel roof.

At Syderstone in north west Norfolk there is a round tower with a west door, the only access to the church. It is thought that this was at one time a cruciform church and there are scars on the outside walls of a former arcade of arches.

Most remaining round towers are in small villages but at Bungay in Suffolk it is in the town. The church has a dormer window. This is one of 42 round towers in Suffolk.

The tallest round tower is at Mutford in Suffolk. Here the height has been increased by the addition of an octagonal belfry. This church, like Syderstone, has a west door.

The largest round tower in diameter in Suffolk is at Wortham which has a much later impressive clerestory.

Not all the round towers are in East Anglia. There is a nice example at Great Shefford in Berkshire.

Of the 42 round towers in Suffolk one of the best is Thorington with Norman blind arcading and a later coronet.

In Gloucestershire there are two churches with a hexagonal tower; in both cases the form is irregular.

At Swindon near Cheltenham the result gives the impression of a bad drawing.

The other example which is at Ozleworth is a central tower in an axial church.

Another hexagonal shape is the west porch at Icklesham in Sussex. The remains of the north transept are still standing, reminiscent of Heacham in Norfolk.

Not hexagonal, but Cartmel Priory in what was Lancashire and is now part of Cumbria has an unusual diagonally-set top to the central tower.

The tower at Clare in Suffolk is a little too small for the size of the church, but in this view from the east it is supported by the tall pinnacles which mark the separation of the chancel from the nave.

The west tower at Newnham in Northamptonshire has arches large enough to allow processions to pass beneath it.

There is another example of the drive-through tower at St Peter Mancroft in Norwich. This tower is topped with a very fine and balanced cupola.

Apsley Guise in Bedfordshire has an unusual tower with west and south entrances.

At Brook near Ashford in Kent the tower has almost the same area as the rest of the church, as it has a first floor chamber within.

Contrast in towers, at Cricklade in Hampshire, late medieval; at Devizes in Wiltshire, Norman.

TOWERS

Northamptonshire, Leicestershire and Rutland all benefited from the availability of good masonry. They have as a consequence fine spires. Gaddesby in Leicestershire is a good example, with windows known as lucarnes spaced up the spire.

# A CHURCH NEAR YOU

The spire of Hemingborough church in Yorkshire is 191 ft. but looks higher because it forms about two thirds of the total height of the steeple.

Essex is not a county of spires but at Thaxted there is a finely balanced design rising to 181 ft.

# TOWERS

Shottesbrooke church has the tallest spire in Berkshire at 185 ft. The church is a perfect cruciform being built all at one time.

The church at Hemel Hempstead in Hertfordshire is also cruciform but is basically Norman. The spire at 200 ft. is the tallest in its county.

The spire on Holy Trinity Church, Southampton, has had a use not foreseen when it was built. Its survival during the blitz on the city during World War II is attributed to its use as a guide for the navigation of enemy bombers. Subsequently, when under repair, at a request from the Admiralty, nine extra feet were added to the height, making it 202 ft.

Short in relation to the tower, the spire at Hanslope is nevertheless the tallest in Buckinghamshire at 186 ft.

Lyddington in Rutland has a foreshortened spire similar to Hanslope but is not diminished as a result.

Winterton-on-Sea near the North Sea coast in Norfolk is a navigation aid and was a look-out post in world War II. At 132 ft. tall it stands proudly as a challenge to the wind farms.

The highly decorated tower of Wheatacre in the south east of Norfolk seems almost frivolous in comparison.

There are two other examples of churches as an aid to navigation in North Norfolk. At 175 ft. the steeple at Snettisham is the tallest in Norfolk outside Norwich and is close to the Wash. The church was originally cruciform and has a fine west window.

Blakeney on the north coast has a subsidiary tower on the side of the chancel; it is thought that it would have contained a light for navigation.

A CHURCH NEAR YOU

A familiar navigation aid on the Blackwater is the tower of Maldon Church in Essex.

In disturbed places the tower of the church was a place of refuge for the population. There are several examples in Herefordshire.

At Ewyas Harold there is a fine construction with an unusual buttress called a clasping buttress, round the south west corner of the tower.

At Bosbury in Herefordshire, near Ledbury, the detached tower has the appearance of a fortress. There was a bishops' palace here once, which probably called for serious protection.

The Scottish border also created hostilities and at Ancroft in Northumberland the peel tower was built to serve as defence and refuge. A large Norman south door survives from a time before the construction of the tower.

The tower at Shalfleet on the Isle of Wight was a refuge, more against the French than the Welsh or Scots.

The broach spire is a clever device for reducing the eight sides of a spire to four, to fit the tower. There are a number in Sussex.

At Billingshurst, Sussex, the spire is the same height as the tower. This is a church with west door access.

Slightly surprisingly there is another at Llanelly near Abergavenny in Monmouthshire. Here there was plenty of sandstone but also plenty of timber.

There is another broach tower in Herefordshire at Fownhope in the south east of the county, on another central towered axial church.

At Westbury-on-Severn in Gloucestershire the broach spire is 153 ft. high on a detached tower built as an observation post. The scars from the gable of a former chapel can be seen on the tower.

# TOWERS

Although most churches were being built in stone from the time leading up to the Conquest, in areas where stone was expensive and timber was abundant, timber churches continued to be built.

And if not the whole church, then the tower or just the belfry. High Halden in Kent has an octagonal ground floor and is entirely timber. Mattingley in Hampshire is timber framed. While Mundon's tower in Essex has a hexagonal timber base. Yateley in Hampshire has a half-timbered tower.

In Gloucestershire there is a fine timbered tower with brick infill at Upleadon.

The timber tower at Michelmersh in Hampshire was originally detached. It is now a south west tower, attached to an aisle with very low 'Sussex style' eaves.

While wooden towers were a feature of Essex and Hampshire, the wooden belfry was much developed in the Welsh border country. At Skenfrith in Monmouthshire, near the Hereford border, there is what is termed a border or Montgomery belfry.

The belfry at Meonstoke in Hampshire is a more sophisticated version.

Towers are not always on a rectangular plan. At Maldon in Essex the street pattern forced the tower of All Saints Church into a triangular form.

At Little Maplestead also in Essex the church is circular in plan. There are four of these in England, inspired by the Church of the Holy Sepulchre in Jerusalem.

# TOWERS

The round church in Cambridge has an octagonal annex. Apart from the round church already noted in Northampton, there is another in London.

The central tower of St Nicholas, Leicester provides a lesson in styles. The lower level of blind arcading is Norman, but the later addition is Gothic, with pointed arches.

A tower can be enhanced with a cupola or even quite simple arrangements such as a weather vane. Lymington in Hampshire is a good example.

Cruciform Aylesbury in Buckinghamshire has had many alterations over time and has another more elaborate example.

TOWERS

Faversham in Kent has a unique style. Originally a central towered cruciform church, the tower collapsed in the 13th century. Much work including the west tower was done in the 19th century.

Tillington in Sussex has what is called a Scottish Crown.

Portsmouth Dockyard Church has an attractive cupola, similar to Lymington.

East Anglia is dominant in producing attractive toppings to towers. Sometimes it is an insignificant addition which serves adequately to fill the space. Diss in Norfolk is an example.

Mattishall in Norfolk has a well balanced tower. It is enhanced enormously by the modest addition.

# TOWERS

Toppesfield with a 17th century church tower in Essex has an attractive development of the more militaristic medieval tower.

Boxford and Little Cornard in Suffolk

Swaffham, Norfolk

The more elaborate East Harling in Norfolk.

The tower at Barley in Hertfordshire received attention from the great Victorian architect, Henry Butterfield. The result adds distinction to an otherwise rather plain tower.

Without a tower a church looks bare, but Inglesham in Wiltshire has a very likeable little church which reveals on the inside perfect 17th and 18th century furnishings. It emphasises one of the drawbacks of this book, that while concentrating on the exterior, many wonderful treasures inside are overlooked. This is a CCT church.

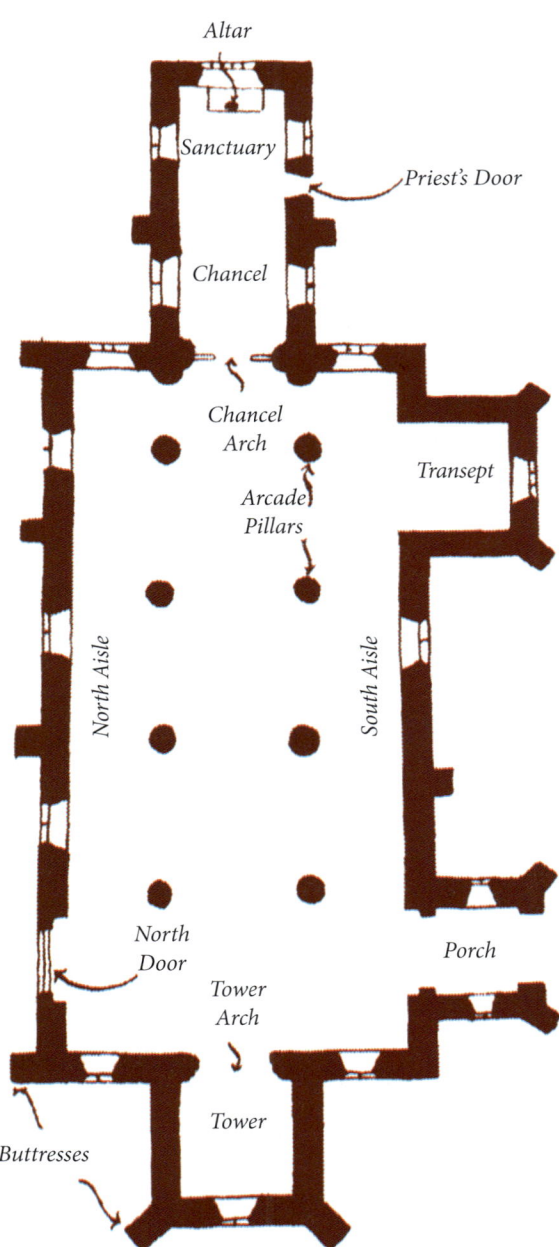

Typical church layout

# Chapter 3: **Layout**

The basic Celtic church layout of nave and square-ended chancel often received a west tower. In fact something like 85% of English churches have a west tower. However the central tower appeared on Continental style axial churches and on the cruciform churches developed by the Normans. These churches in some counties served as a local headquarters for the establishing of parishes and were called minsters. As a result, in parts of southern England important towns have central towered churches. Bedford has three of them.

However the central tower in a cruciform church, if supported on four arches rather than the ground, was liable to collapse. As a result there are a number of cases where the tower has moved from being central to another part of the church, normally to the west end. There are only three cases where the central tower was kept when a west tower was built. Among those who lost the central tower, evidence of its existence may be more or less disguised.

There are also examples of where the tower was placed elsewhere on the church, while in parts of East Anglia and in Herefordshire, there are towers totally detached from the church. This could be due to the softness of the ground, but in more unruly parts of the country it was their role to be a refuge from attack.

Where towers appeared in other parts of the church, it is sometimes hard to tell the reason. There are however a number of locations where a reason is fairly obvious, the site being limited, either by streets or the fall of the land.

There are three cases where a west tower was added without first demolishing the central tower. The church at Wimborne in Dorset, a minster church, has a second tower at the west end and the central tower remains. The church was built with two colours of masonry.

Old Clee church between Grimsby and Cleethorpes in Lincolnshire retained its central tower when the west tower was built.

Purton in Wiltshire is another church with a central tower and also a west tower.

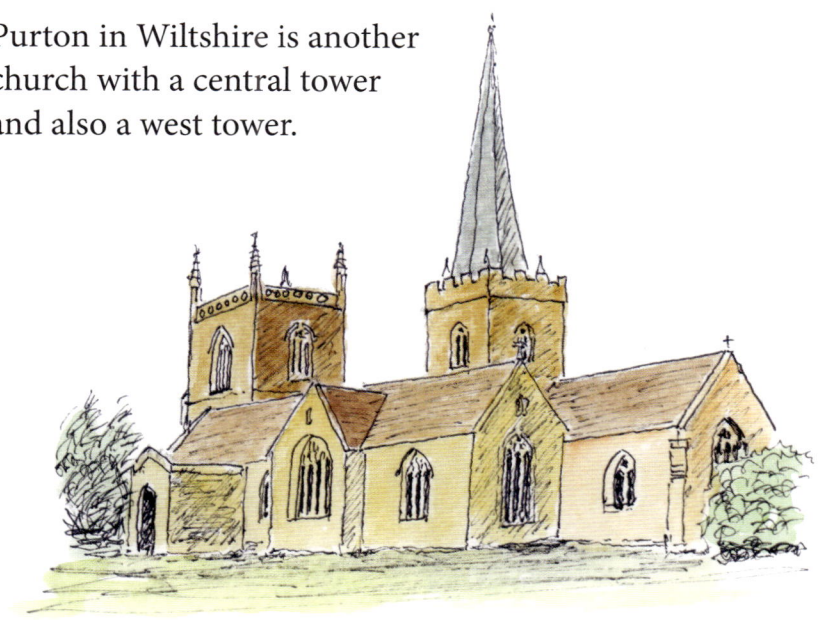

Ottery St Mary in Devon is cruciform but has no central tower. Instead it has two towers built on the transepts, said to be in imitation of Exeter Cathedral.

Abingdon in Oxfordshire has a north tower as the site is constrained. So confined was it that expansion was sideways, southward from an initial nave and north aisle. This nave became another north aisle when the main nave was built. Later two south aisles were added.

Bicester in Oxfordshire has a church which once had a central tower. it is still possible to make out where it was.

At Melksham in Wiltshire the central tower was pulled down and a west tower erected in the 19th century. These sketches demonstrate the church before and after.

All Saints, Leicester was on a busy road. It is thought that the tower was originally detached; it now stands on the north side of the church near the east end.

Whether through the need to improve access or to resolve the result of losing part of a church, there are two very similar solutions in widely separated parts of the country.

At Garway in Herefordshire, the defensive towers was a originally detached from the church and is now linked by a covered passage.

At Holme-next-the-Sea in Norfolk, when the south aisle was pulled down, the tower, which also served as a south porch, was separated from the remaining nave. A passageway was built to connect them.

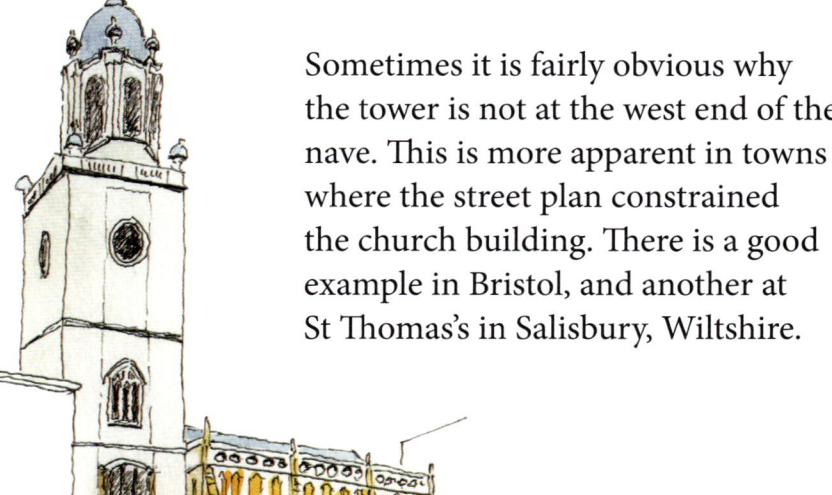

Sometimes it is fairly obvious why the tower is not at the west end of the nave. This is more apparent in towns where the street plan constrained the church building. There is a good example in Bristol, and another at St Thomas's in Salisbury, Wiltshire.

St Stephen's in Norwich is at the top of a steep slope. The tower had to be placed on the north side.

There was good reason at Exton in Somerset to put the tower on the south side before the slope steepens.

At Huntingdon, Cambridgeshire, the church is in the crowded town centre and there is a north tower.

At Stapleford in Wiltshire it may have been the downward slope of the land at the west end that caused the tower to be built on the north side.

In Oxford the 'dreamiest' of spires is on a north tower on the University Church. Built around 1270, it is in the Decorated style, a more sophisticated Gothic than Early English which preceded it, and which the Victorians called 'First pointed'.

Castleton in Oxfordshire has a south tower, and an amazingly low pitched roof on the north aisle.

LAYOUT

In the middle of Stamford, Lincolnshire, the site of All Saints Church is surrounded by streets and the church had to build the tower on the north side.

At Needham Market in Suffolk, among a number of unusual features, the tower is over the south porch. A clerestory sits on top of the nave roof.

# A CHURCH NEAR YOU

At Eling on Southampton Water the site is constrained.

At Cucklington in Gloucestershire the church is on the side of a steep hill.

At South Ferriby near the Humber river in Lincolnshire the church is on a very steep slope. In the 19th century the nave was re-aligned north/south and a chancel was built on the west end, giving this church a very unusual layout.

Cawood in Yorkshire was too close to the River Ouse to build a west tower.

At Wawne near Hull in the East Riding the church stands on relatively high ground in a marshy area. It is likely that the site was limited for this reason.

At Wrotham in Kent the site was too close to the main road.

There is no obvious reason for the position of the tower at Kington in Herefordshire, though it stands on a hill.

Even more puzzling is why Pembridge (also in Herefordshire) has a detached tower when standing high and dry on a hill. The layered spire is typical in the county.

The church at Old Hunstanton, Norfolk, was enlarged in the 19th century and what had been the nave became the north aisle. As a result the tower became north west.

At Calne in Wiltshire the central tower fell in 1638 and a north tower was built on the north transept. To have placed it at the west end would have blocked a west window.

At Corsham in Wiltshire, to erect a tower at the west end of the nave would have interfered with the riding stables of the nearby manor.

At Great Chalfield in Wiltshire the church was an easy step from the great house and a turret served to accommodate the bell.

# Chapter 4: **Enhancement**

The basic Celtic pattern served well for many churches, but as early as the Saxon period there were examples of a structure at the sides of the main nave. The easiest way to expand the capacity of a church was to build sideways. From the 13th century a number of chancels were extended, but this was for ritualistic reasons. Aisles on one or both sides of the nave tended to reduce the light in the nave. A solution was to create windows in the nave wall, above the arcade separating the nave from the aisle, a clerestory. These were necessarily small in order to preserve the stability of the structure. Until lead sheeting was available to make a low-pitched roof for the aisle, a lean-to aisle roof also placed limitations on the size of clerestory windows. (See Havant). Raising the height of the nave roof was an expensive solution. Another solution was to construct a gabled roof over the aisle. This had the drawback of creating a gully between the nave and the aisle, where dead leaves and water tended to collect in what could become a church-warden's nightmare. But it did allow large windows in the aisle.

The period after the Black Death in 1350 saw a big change in English church architecture. The large windows, with low arches of the Perpendicular style, spread from Gloucester Cathedral to those parts of the country enjoying the increasing wealth of the wool trade. Suffolk, Gloucestershire and Somerset especially saw dramatic church expansion with large areas of window.

In counties where there was plentiful timber and masonry was scarce, there was a tendency to build large roofs and for their eaves to come near to the ground, with a continuous slope over both nave and aisle. This was particularly the case in Sussex. There is a charming example at Berwick near Lewes in East Sussex, which is also rich in wall paintings.

Grosmont in Monmouthshire, another cruciform church, has similar low eaves, with extra light from a dormer window. It also has an octagonal tower.

ENHANCEMENT

At Tong in Kent near Sittingbourne the low eaves, the south porch and tower obscured the light.

On the north side dormer windows were installed as a solution.

A similar sloping aisle roof can be found at Barton in Westmorland, Cumbria, on an axial central towered church.

Climping on the Sussex coast has a 'Sussex roof' over the north aisle of a Saxon nave. The tower is on the south transept.

# ENHANCEMENT

Outside Sussex there are other examples of the long sloping roof and low eaves, one in Northamptonshire at Great Oakley, another in Oxfordshire at Newnham Murren, and another with a clerestory in Berkshire at Wallingford.

Aldeburgh church on the coast of Suffolk offers the other extreme. The south aisle has large windows and there is no clerestory. This is possible because the roof of the aisle is nearly flat. Halifax church in Yorkshire demonstrates the position with and without a clerestory.

# ENHANCEMENT

The ultimate in clerestories is perhaps Long Melford in Suffolk, which is a beautifully proportioned church. There are 16 windows each side and the Suffolk tower stands amiably at one end.

The largest church in England is at Kingston on Hull, Yorkshire. The immense clerestory extends for the whole length of the church. This church is also notable for the extensive use of brick, made economic by proximity to the Humber.

Sherborne Abbey in Dorset, another large cruciform church with central tower, has exceptionally large clerestory windows.

ENHANCEMENT

Blythburgh near the Suffolk coast appears to be nearly all glass. Chipping Norton in Oxfordshire goes even further at clerestory level, but is surprisingly subdued at a lower level.

127

After 1350 the wealth of the country grew, not only in the counties with major wool production. Thus Basingstoke in Hampshire and Newbury in Berkshire saw expansion of their churches. The latter was enhanced by a 'gothick' archway.

In East Anglia the style was widespread with examples in even small villages. Denton in Suffolk has one of these, a lovely church but too large for the population. Shelton in Norfolk is similar and even has a parvise.

Warminster in Wiltshire has a long clerestory.

The church at Ewelme in Oxfordshire looks as though it should be in East Anglia. This is because the granddaughter of Chaucer who lived there, married the Duke of Suffolk.

Sometimes the clerestory looks foreshortened when installed in a small church. Mentmore in Buckinghamshire is an example. There is another at Glatton in Cambridgeshire.

At Bodenham in Herefordshire the erection of a spire was not completed. This is another church with a long sloping roof over the south aisle, leaving low eaves and little space for the clerestory.

At Pilton in Somerset there is a fine clerestory but no aisle.

At Crowcombe in the same county there is no clerestory but large aisle windows.

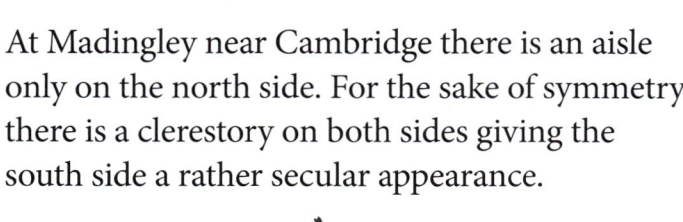

At Madingley near Cambridge there is an aisle only on the north side. For the sake of symmetry there is a clerestory on both sides giving the south side a rather secular appearance.

ENHANCEMENT

The advantage of a nearly flat aisle roof as at Aldeburgh is that it is not necessary to raise the nave roof in order to find room for a clerestory. If on the other hand the roof of the aisle is sloped, the result is either small windows in the clerestory or a high nave roof. Trellech in Monmouthshire is a good example of this.

In Sussex, a county with relatively few clerestories, Steyning provides another example.

133

The result of a sloping aisle roof and avoiding raising the nave roof can be seen at Kilmington in Wiltshire.

Langford in Bedfordshire demonstrates the advantage of a low pitched roof on the aisle.

The gabled aisle roof provides an easier solution, avoiding having to raise the nave roof, and still providing enough space for good aisle windows. Holdenby in Northamptonshire is an example. As is Bisham in Berkshire, by the Thames.

# A CHURCH NEAR YOU

Dyrham in Gloucestershire demonstrates how large a window can be obtained by using a gabled aisle.

ENHANCEMENT

Two churches in Oxfordshire serve to compare the effect of a sloping aisle roof and a gabled aisle, Stanton St John and Hook Norton.

The lowest cost solution to providing more light is the dormer window. This has been used in later years and in some cases it has been an attractive solution. One of the best is at Mavis Enderby in Lincolnshire.

A simple solution is at Kirby Underdale in Yorkshire.

# ENHANCEMENT

Dormer windows can be an eyesore but there are some cleverly discreet examples. Burnham on Crouch in Essex has battlements on the wall of the south aisle which restrict the sight of the dormers. While the thatched church at Beighton in Norfolk is actually improved by the dormers.

Where there is an aisle on only one side of a nave, churches may have a totally different appearance on each side.

Little Sampford in north west Essex is one example. Here the north side is the side of approach and the south side is bare.

At Piddinghoe near Lewes in Sussex the round towered church has a clerestory only on the south side. The low eaves are still there but the long slope of the Sussex roof is broken by the clerestory.

Expansion of a church normally led to distinct functions, with the nave the main part of the church. However at Bedwellty in western Monmouthshire, high above the industrial valleys, the church has a north aisle of similar size to the nave, and uniquely the altar is at the end of the arcade separating them.

On the other hand at Pakefield near Lowestoft, Suffolk, two churches side by side were eventually joined, though the altar is at the end of only one of the naves.

An opportunistic layout was to build a church in the city walls. Two of these survive, one in Bristol and the other in Winchester.

ENHANCEMENT

At Frome in Somerset there is a very un-English enhancement in the form of a *via crucis* (way of the cross), leading up to the church, which itself has an unusual layout.

Until the 19th century many churches were rendered and whitewashed or painted. A few still are, mainly in Wales. In the 19th century it became fashionable to reveal the raw materials of which churches were made, many of which had little colour. There were however examples of churches where the stone used in the fabric was itself colourful, and uses of more than one colour produced striped effects. One of the largest examples is at Cliffe in Kent.

Another is at Fingringhoe in Essex.

Tempsford in Bedfordshire is more exotic being a combination of more colourful stones.

In the same county Luton has an alternative pattern, equally striking.

# Chapter 5: **Doorways**

In the Celtic style of church it was the custom in England to enter a church on the south or north side. Originally this was because the colder north side of a church was regarded as the Devil's side and, at the moment of Baptism, he needed a door through which to escape. Later one or other of these doors was less used and was in some cases blocked up. This normally left the south door as the main door, but if principal access to the church was from the north, it was the north door which became the main entrance.

Another English characteristic is the porch. This may be derived from the Anglo-Saxon porticus as seen at Brixworth. It may have been prompted by the weather, but it became a useful space for meetings and weddings. If an upper storey was built, called a parvise, it provided in some cases accommodation for the curate, and more often became a useful place to put things.

Another English peculiarity is the apparent reluctance to use a west door. On the Continent, in non-conformist chapels, and in English cathedrals and abbeys with twin west towers, it is normal to enter the church at the west end. A reason for this exception may be that, with a bell or bells in the west tower, the entrance would have been obstructed by bell ringers. As a result there are churches where the bells are rung from an upper chamber.

The position was complicated in the 19th century by The Ecclesiastical Society who campaigned for order in church services. They advocated bell ringers being on the ground floor so that they would be more visible and less inclined to slip away to the pub.

Most English cathedrals and abbeys have or had twin towers. King's Lynn church was a Minster and has twin towers though of different dates. The south tower is Early English Gothic 'pointed style'. The north tower and windows are of the Perpendicular style, post 1350. There is a west door and it is the principal entrance.

Bourne Abbey church in Lincolnshire was originally intended to have twin towers and therefore has a west door.

St Germans in Cornwall, a Grade 1 listed Norman priory church, was built in the early 1200s as part of an Augustinian Priory on the site of the county's first cathedral.

The apparent prejudice against using the west door (if there is one) is more likely to be overcome if the west end of the church is facing the street. St George's Church in Stamford Lincolnshire is an example of this.

At Standon in Hertfordshire the church was built on a steep slope leading down to a busy road. This may account for the west door, and the detached tower.

In the centre of Sleaford in Lincolnshire the west door opens onto the market place. Although the bells had been rung from the ground floor until 2003, the west door has been the main entrance. They are now rung from an upper chamber.

At Campsall near Doncaster in Yorkshire the main door is on the south side of the nave, but the west door has wheelchair access and the bells are rung from an upper room.

The Abbey at Bath, now the parish church, is cruciform. Here the west door opens onto a principal space in the middle of the city.

In Cambridge St Botolph opens directly onto the street through the west door. The north and south doors have been blocked off.

In Wisbech, Cambridgeshire, there was limited space to the west and a west tower was demolished. The present tower is a north tower, and although there is a west door, the main entrance is a south door under the parvise.

This church has had a complex history. The existing west door was the entrance from the original nave into a west tower. The church expanded southward as that was the only vacant space. Subsequently the north and south aisles and north tower were built. As a result there are three arcades of arches within the body of the church.

An unusual little church can be found at Otford near Sevenoaks in Kent. It has a number of rare features. For a start it is rendered and painted white. Although many churches were at one time painted or whitewashed, it became fashionable in the 19th century to reveal the materials in the fabric. Secondly it has a west door in use as the main entrance, with a small porch. Furthermore the bells are still rung from the ground floor, thus confounding the theory. Finally there is an odd little spire with the belfry openings let into it.

Rotherwas Chapel in Herefordshire has another example of a west door. It also has an interesting little cupola on top of the spire. Like the church at Kempley it is owned by English Heritage

Roos near the North Sea coast in Yorkshire has a significant west porch and the west door is the entrance. The bells are rung from an upper level.

At Bottisham in Cambridgeshire there is a somewhat grander west porch with a tall arch which has been filled in. This size of west porch is termed a Galilee. There is some suggestion that it is modelled on Ely Cathedral. It is no longer in use and entrance is now through a south door.

Cuddesdon in Oxfordshire also has a proper west porch, and a south porch as well.

Abergavenny in Monmouthshire, another cruciform church, has what is termed a narthex at the west entrance.

Another cruciform church with west door and large porch is at Llantilio Crossenny in Monmouthshire.

The central tower was relatively common in this county, perhaps because of the strong Norman presence. This spire is an 18th century addition.

# DOORWAYS

At Lyme Regis in Dorset the west porch is in fact the former nave. The tower was central and to increase capacity a new nave was built to the east of it. The English affection for porches seems to be fairly insistent.

The west porch at Lacock in Wiltshire is more modest, while that at Maids Moreton in Buckinghamshire is stylish if minimal. There are however north and south doors as well.

The west porch at Great Wakering in Essex has a parvise and at Langley Marish in Buckinghamshire the stylish west porch is at the end of the nave.

At Lydd in Kent there are two west doors but no porch. The tower at 132 ft. is one of the tallest in the county.

# DOORWAYS

Calbourne on the Isle of Wight has a west door with a small porch on the end of the nave. The tower is on the south side, possibly because the church was originally cruciform.

The other Essex spire is at Saffron Walden where the west door is the main entrance. The bells are rung from an upper chamber. There are also gabled aisles.

# A CHURCH NEAR YOU

Where the church has a central tower there is less reason for avoiding a west door entrance, yet few exist. There is an exception at Long Crendon in Buckinghamshire, and another at North Perrot in Somerset. South Perrot, which is across the county boundary in Dorset, is also cruciform and also has a west door and porch.

The oldest Sussex churches are near the coast as the hinterland was dense forest. Broadwater, around which Worthing has developed, has a cruciform church on Saxon foundations. It has a west door and a porch which is decorated with flint flushwork like churches in East Anglia.

North and south doors have yielded some extravagant porches, and there is great variety. At Great Massingham in Norfolk there is a fine display of Early English style Gothic windows along the sides. While at Meesden in Hertfordshire the porch dominates the little church.

The building of an upper chamber or parvise provided an opportunity for great extravagance. Many of these are fairly simple like the one at Great Shelford near Cambridge. A more lavish alternative is at Hitchin in Hertfordshire.

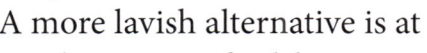

At Garboldisham in Norfolk the west porch was moved to the north side, perhaps because of the installation of bells, and the result is an elaborate East Anglian type of porch with flint flush-work.

There is a better example of this with a parvise at Southwold in Suffolk.

In the Fenland of west Norfolk there are some superb churches. West Walton is one of them and it has a fine porch.

Nayland in Suffolk has an odd south porch with the doorway facing west. This may be due to the proximity of the street.

At Coddenham in Suffolk the north porch, which is the normal point of entry, has been partially rotated from the line of the church in order to face directly up the path from the village.

Syresham in Northamptonshire has a modest south porch distinguished by its west facing entrance.

South Newington in Oxfordshire is a handsome example, greatly enhanced by the colourful stone.

Pulham St Mary in the south of Norfolk has a striking appearance with a parvise.

At Leverington in the north of Cambridgeshire the porch is superbly elegant, dignified but not flamboyant. The tower has what are termed gabled buttresses, more decorative than functional.

For magnificence Cirencester, Gloucestershire, wins every time. So large is the porch that it was for a time used as the Town Hall.

At Radwinter in Essex there is an elegant timber framed porch with a rather West Country appearance.

Burford in Oxfordshire presents a strong contrast with a parvise on two levels.

For beauty, balance and artistry the north porch at Thaxted, Essex, is hard to beat.

# Chapter 6: **Casualties**

Churches in England have changed over the centuries. partly as we have seen due to expansion and increased wealth, but partly for negative reasons. In counties such as Norfolk without good masonry, where the normal construction material had to be flint or rubble, the fabric needed constant maintenance. The introduction of change-ringing in about 1600 put pressure on the fabric of towers and called for extra buttressing; the forces generated by eight heavy bells rotating back and forth at some height are considerable. Mention has already been made of the vulnerability of central towers. Malmesbury offers an example of excessive pride and rivalry leading to collapse.

Other changes have been brought about by earth movement, and by coastal changes, erosion as much as silting of harbours, and a number of churches have been deserted by their village, due to pandemics such as the Black Death.

There have been other causes of change, more man-made. The Reformation brought about the deliberate destruction of parts of a number of churches. The chancel was the principal victim, but transepts also suffered. The Civil War in the 17th century led to massive damage in parts of the country, especially in Yorkshire. World War II affected mainly cities.

Finally, closure of a church leaving it to cope with sun, wind, rain and vandals, can lead to its gradual deterioration. It still calls out for care.

An extreme case of earth movement caused the church at Cwmyoy in Monmouthshire to be seriously contorted. While the nave remains upright, the chancel and tower lean sharply in opposite directions. The tower is held up by massive buttresses.

At Botolphs in Sussex the harbour silted up over time, the population declined and the north aisle was removed. the marks of the arches in the arcade remain in the north wall of the nave.

Sometimes movement of population preserves the integrity of a church, saving it from excessive 'restoration'. Hamsey near Lewes in East Sussex is an example. It has only one house as a neighbour but is well cared for.

Sometimes it has been possible to make a virtue out of a disaster. At Hemingford Grey in Cambridgeshire near Huntingdon a storm struck the spire in 1707. The remains were tidied up, given a coronet, and have survived quite successfully.

Bawdsey on the Suffolk coast suffered silting of the harbour and a population decline. The south aisle was removed.

Ranworth Church on the Norfolk Broads bears the scars from the removal of a north aisle.

# A CHURCH NEAR YOU

Church towers often need support from buttresses. This may be because of weak ground or poor quality building materials. Since change ringing began in around 1600, the forces let loose on a tower by the rotating of heavy bells has been another cause. There was a particularly serious need at Conington, Cambridgeshire, with a different resolution at Brasted in Kent, where the west door arch is incorporated in a buttress. The low tower and heavy buttresses at Laverton in Somerset suggest unstable ground.

Similar to the position at Brasted are two oddities in Norfolk. In each case a buttress terminates on the arch of a doorway.

Warham

Trunch

At Much Cowarne in Herefordshire the position may have been unstable, perched on a hill. Ticehurst in East Sussex had less of a problem, solved by so-called angled buttresses.

Balsham in Cambridgeshire is on firm ground so it must have been the materials which led to such serious buttressing of the tower.

Burmarsh in Kent have a robust character suggesting that much force was needed.

# A CHURCH NEAR YOU

In the 17th century it was decided that Covehithe in Suffolk had a church which was too large. So a smaller one was built inside, just as was done at Pontefract. The old building has survived its proximity to the North Sea and, so far, has escaped coastal erosion, which is bringing the sea ever closer.

The Reformation prevented the completion of the tower at East Bergholt in Suffolk. Instead there is a detached bell tower.

At Abbey Dore in Herefordshire the Reformation led to the destruction of most of the nave. Later a new tower was placed in the angle between the surviving chancel and the south transept.

Another victim of the Reformation was Crowland Abbey in Lincolnshire. The surviving tower is the former north west tower of what was once a cruciform church with a central tower.

St Mary's Priory, Old Malton in Yorkshire has lost its north tower. It still has the west door associated with twin tower churches.

While Marsh Baldon near Oxford is an example of failed plans to build a spire leading to a truncated octagon. It also has an unusual entrance through a west door in a north aisle.

# A CHURCH NEAR YOU

Old Bolingbroke church in Lincolnshire was a victim of the Civil War. The tower was a normal west tower on the nave, but both nave and chancel were destroyed by gunfire and explosives. The original south aisle became the nave and later a narrow north aisle was added. The tower thus became a north west tower.

Pamber in Hampshire was a cruciform priory chapel. Only the tower and chancel have survived. The south wall of the old nave is still partially in existence.

CASUALTIES

Among man-made casualties is Reculver in Kent. The ancient foundation was being demolished in 1807 as obsolete when the Admiralty stepped in to save the towers, for navigation purposes.

No single event led to the collapse of the north transept at Heacham in west Norfolk, but inferior materials, probably combined with a lack of maintenance, played a part.

Malmesbury Abbey, Wiltshire, now the parish church, suffered one of the most calamitous histories of any English church. A Norman building with central tower, the abbot was determined that it should be taller than Salisbury cathedral. The objective was achieved at 431 ft, against the 404 ft of Salisbury, However nemesis came in 1507 when a storm caused the tower to collapse and ruin a transept and much of the nave. A new tower was built at the west end and this too collapsed in about 1550, destroying more of the nave. Part of the nave and a splendid south porch survive.

# CASUALTIES

Two spires in Kent suffered damage from the weather. The responses by the parishes differed. Hackington was more adventurous.

At Chislet, the spire on the central tower was simply cut off.

At Little Walsingham in Norfolk the church was seriously damaged by fire. Only the tower and south porch survived. It was meticulously restored.

When Great Walsingham lost its chancel it was not replaced.

Hardly a casualty, more a survivor is the church at Dry Donnington between Newark and Grantham, in Lincolnshire. The tower leans 5.1 degrees from the vertical compared with the mere 3.9 degrees at Pisa.

The church at East Shefford in Berkshire was closed in 1870 re-opened in 1887, and closed again in 1958.
It is now a CCT church.

Another Civil War victim was Scarborough. What at first sight appears to be a west tower is in fact the surviving central tower now serving as the chancel.

A similar result was reached without the same excuse at Flitcham in west Norfolk, where part of the south transept survives. The originally central tower is now the chancel. The same happened at Dallinghoo in Suffolk.

Old St Nicholas at Uphill near Weston-super-Mare in Somerset was closed in 1846. It is now part-ruined and cared for by the CCT.

Crondall in Hampshire has had a series of mishaps. It had a central tower which collapsed. A west tower was built to replace it. That too fell and a north east tower was built in a position where a tower is rarely found. The nave is heavily buttressed.

The priory church at Wymondham in Norfolk has suffered greatly from time and mankind. It was originally cruciform with a central tower and two west towers. The central tower and transepts collapsed. They were replaced by what was then a new central tower. Later the twin west towers were demolished and replaced by a single west tower 142 ft. tall. In the Reformation the chancel was demolished.

The sketch below illustrated the process looking towards the east. The solid lines are what survives today with west tower, aisled nave, and the new central tower with an octagonal top. The dotted lines illustrate the original with twin west towers, a central tower, transepts and chancel.

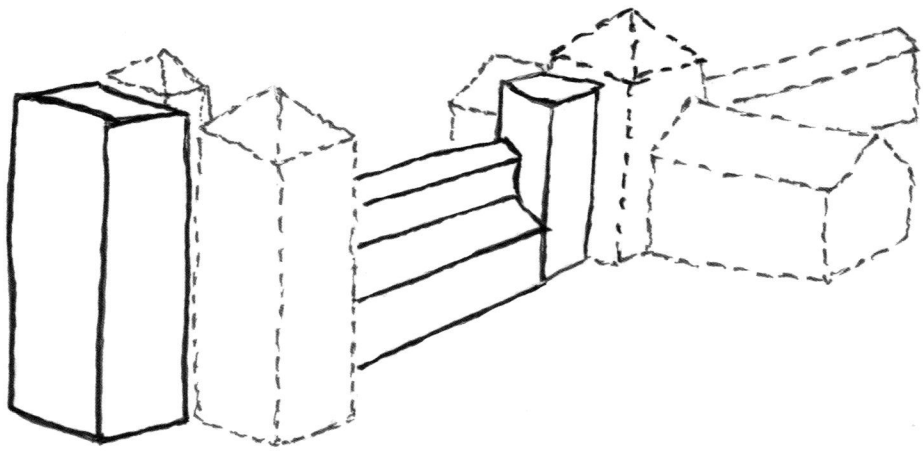

This view of the church today is from the east with in the foreground the remains of the central tower and the arch to the nave. In the background is the single west tower.

Sometimes the repair of a church alters its character. At Ingworth in Norfolk what looks like a west apse is in fact the base of a collapsed round tower.

At East Barsham in Norfolk the north tower has been reduced to a porch.

This church at Stanton in Suffolk became redundant in 1756. A roofless ruin, it is preserved by the CCT.

Springs and rabbits caused the church at Boughton in Northamptonshire to crumble. This is how it appeared in the 18th century. It has deteriorated further since then.

# A CHURCH NEAR YOU

The old church at Bix in Oxfordshire was abandoned in 1875, as the population centre had moved away and a new church had been built. Judging by the size of the surviving buttress the church was in trouble before it was deserted.

Tilney cum Islington church, cruciform but with a west tower, served a scattered community in the rich fenlands of western Norfolk. The lead on the nave roof was stolen in the 1970s and the church became redundant. It is managed by the CCT.

# A CHURCH NEAR YOU

At Llanwarne in Herefordshire there is a large deserted church. 'Llanwarne' means 'church in a marsh' in Welsh and this was the problem. In 1864, after suffering rising water levels for 500 years, a decision was made to build a new church on higher ground.

On a more cheerful note, the church at Corton, north of Lowestoft in Suffolk, still functions as a church in spite of a weakened tower and no roof on part of the nave. This part of the nave now has a small garden and the rest of the nave and the chancel serve as the church.

The church at Hargham near Attleborough in Norfolk has had a history with a happy ending. During the 18th century the tower collapsed into the nave and the church was deserted. In the 20th century local people took an initiative, revived the church and put it in order. It now accommodates occasional services and is in the care of the Norfolk Churches Trust.

# CASUALTIES

The church at Waterden in Norfolk is witness to the powers of survival, if there is a helping hand. Having lost its tower and south aisle, not to mention the population of its village, it was saved by the Norfolk Churches Trust. Alone in the countryside with only the former Rectory for company, it is now under the wing of South Creake, a neighbouring parish. Occasional services are held and it is open to visitors and even has its own car park, fenced off in a corner of a field.

# Index *Locations listed by county*

**BEDFORDSHIRE**
Apsley Guise, *St Botolph* 75
Bedford, *St Mary* 24
Clapham, *St Thomas* 18
Duntstable, *Duntstable Abbey* 39
Felmersham, *St Mary* 39
Langford, *St Andrew* 134
Luton, *St Mary* 145
Tempsford, *St Peter* 145

**BERKSHIRE**
Bisham, *All Saints* 135
East Garston, *All Saints* 29
East Shefford, *St Thomas'* 191
Great Shefford, *St Mary* 71
Newbury, *St Nicolas* 128
Shottesbrook, *St John the Baptist* 79
Upton cum Chalvey, Slough,
  *St Laurence* 21
Wallingford, *St Mary le More* 123
Wickham, *St Swithun* 18

**BUCKINGHAMSHIRE**
Aylesbury, *St Mary the Virgin* 94
Beaconsfield, *St Mary & All Saints* 53
Hanslope, *St James the Great* 80
Langley Marish, *St Mary* 158
Long Crendon, *St Mary* 160
Maids Moreton, *St Edmunds* 157
Mentmore, *St Mary* 131
Stewkley *St Michael & All Angels* 24
Wing, *All Saints* 47

**CAMBRIDGESHIRE**
Balsham, *Holy Trinity* 181
Bluntisham, *St Mary* 44
Bottisham, *Holy Trinity* 154
Cambridge, *St Benet* 12
Cambridge, *St Botolph* 151
Cambridge, *The Round Church* 93

Conington, *All Saints* 178
Duxford, *St John* 20
Glatton, *St Nicholas* 131
Great Shelford, *St Mary* 163
Hemingford Grey, *St James* 176
Huntingdon, *All Saints* 109
Leverington, *St Leonards* 168
Madingley, *St Mary Magdalene* 132
Mildenhall, *St Mary* 51
Sutton in the Isle, *St Andrew* 66
Swaffham Prior, *St Mary & St Cyriac* 59
Wisbech, *St Peter & St Paul* 152

**CORNWALL**
St Germans, *St German's Priory* 148

**CUMBRIA**
Barton, Westmorland, *St Michael* 122
Cartmel, *Cartmel Priory* 73

**DEVON**
Ottery St Mary, *St Mary* 103

**DORSET**
Lyme Regis, *St Michael the Archangel* 157
Sherborne, *Sherborne Abbey* 126
Wimborne, *Wimborne Minster* 102

**COUNTY DURHAM**
Monkwearmouth, Durham, *St Peter* 17

**ESSEX**
Bradwell-on-Sea, *St Peter-on-the-Wall* 10
Burnham on Crouch, *St Mary* 139
Colchester, *All Saints* 15
Fingringhoe, *St Andrew* 144
Great Wakering, *St Nicholas* 158
Greensted, *St Andrew* 10
Hockley, *St Peter & St Paul* 65
Little Maplestead, *St John the Baptist* 92
Little Sampford, *St Mary the Virgin* 140
Langford, *St Giles* 42

# INDEX

Maldon, *St Mary the Virgin* 84
Maldon, *All Saints* 92
Mundon, *St Mary* 89
Pentlow, *St Gregory & St George* 42
Radwinter, *St Mary the Virgin* 170
Saffron Walden, *St Mary the Virgin* 159
Thaxted, *St John the Baptist* 78, 171
Toppesfield, *St Margaret of Antioch* 97
Upleadon, *St Mary the Virgin* 90

**GLOUCESTERSHIRE**
Chedworth, *St Andrew* 4
Cirencester, *St John the Baptist* 169
Coln St Denis, *St James* 21
Cucklington, *St Lawrence* 112
Deerhurst, *St Mary* 16
Duntisbourne Rouse, *St Michael* 41
Dyrham, *St Peter* 136
Gloucester, *St Mary de Lode* 26
Hewelsfield, *St Mary Magdalene* 26
Kempley, Forest of Dean, *St Mary* 41
Minchinhampton, *Holy Trinity* 65
Ozleworth, *St Nicholas of Myra* 72
Swindon, Cheltenham, *St Lawrence* 72
Tewkesbury, *Tewkesbury Abbey* 36
Westbury on Severn, *St Peter & St Paul* 88

**HAMPSHIRE**
Basingstoke, *St Michael* 128
Calbourne, Isle of Wight, *All Saints* 159
Christchurch, *Christchurch Abbey* 38
Cricklade, *St Sampson* 76
Crondall, *All Saints* 193
East Meon, *All Saints* 33
Eling, Southampton, *St Mary the Virgin* 112
Havant, *St Faith* 31
Lymington, *St Thomas* 94
Mattingley 89
Meonstoke, *St Andrew* 91
Michelmersh, *St Mary* 90
Pamber, *Pamber Priory* 186

Portchester, Portsmouth, *St Mary's* 31
Portsmouth, *Dockyard Church* 95
Shalfleet, Isle of Wight, *St Michael the Archangel* 86
Southampton, *Holy Trinity* 80
Winchester, *St Cross* 32
Winchester, *St Swithin-upon-Kingsgate* 142
Yateley, *St Peter* 89

**HEREFORDSHIRE**
Abbey Dore, *Dore Abbey* 183
Bodenham, *St Michael & All Angels* 131
Bosbury, *Holy Trinity* 85
Bromyard, *St Peter* 30
Ewyas Harold, *St Michael & All Angels* 85
Fownhope, *St Mary* 88
Garway, *St Michael* 106
Kilpeck, *St Mary & St David* 40
Kington, *St Mary* 115
Llanwarne, *St John the Baptist* 200
Madley, *Nativity of The Blessed Virgin Mary* 44
Much Cowarne, *St Mary the Virgin* 180
Pembridge, *St Mary the Virgin* 115
Rotherwas, *Rotherwas Chapel* 153

**HERTFORDSHIRE**
Barley, *St Margaret of Antioch* 98
Hemel Hempstead, *St Mary* 79
Hitchin, *St Mary* 163
Meesden, *St Mary* 162
Pirton, *St Mary* 27
Standon, *St Mary* 149

**KENT**
Barfrestone, *St Nicholas* 40
Brasted, *St Martin* 178
Brook, *St Mary* 76
Burmarsh, *All Saints* 181
Chislet, *St Mary the Virgin* 189
Cliffe-on-Sea, *St Helen* 144
Cliffe-on-Sea, *St Margaret's* 34
Dover, *St Mary in Castro* 32

205

Etchingham, *The Assumption of Blessed Mary & St Nicholas* 23
Faversham, *St Mary of Charity* 95
Hackington, *St Stephen* 189
High Halden, *St Mary the Virgin* 89
Lydd, *All Saints* 158
Milton Regis, *Holy Trinity* 52
New Romney, *St Nicholas* 52
Otford, Sevenoaks, *St Bartholomew* 153
Reculver, *St Mary* 187
Sandwich, *St Peter* 37
Sutton by Dover, *St Peter & St Paul* 45
Tong, *St Giles* 121
Worth, *St Peter & St Paul* 46
Wrotham, *St George* 114

## LEICESTERSHIRE
Gaddesby, *St Luke* 77
Leicester, *All Saints* 105
Leicester, *St Nicholas* 93

## LINCOLNSHIRE
Barton on Humber, *St Peter* 12
Boston, *St Botolph* 58
Bourne, *Bourne Abbey* 148
Crowland, *Crowland Abbey* 184
Dry Donnington, Newark, *St James* 191
Grantham, *St Wulfram* 57
Lincoln, *St Mary-le-Wigford* 11
Louth, *St James* 57
Mavis Enderby, *St Michael* 138
Old Bolingbroke, *St Peter & St Paul* 186
Old Clee, *St Mary the Virgin* 102
Sleaford, *St Denys* 150
Stamford, All Saints 111
Stamford, *St George's* 149
South Ferriby, *St Nicholas* 113
Stow in Lindsey, *Minster Church of St Mary* 32
Waithe, *St Martin* 33

## LONDON
East Ham, *St Mary Magdalene* 43

## MONMOUTHSHIRE
Abergavenny, *Priory Church of St Mary* 155
Bedwellty *St Sannan* 141
Cwmyoy, *St Martin* 174
Grosmont, *St Nicholas* 120
Llanelly, *St Elli* 87
Llantilio Crosseny, *St Teilo* 156
Magor, *St Mary* 28
Portskewett, *St Mary* 45
Skenfrith, *St Bridget* 91
Trellech, *St Nicholas* 133

## NORFOLK
Beighton, *St Mary the Virgin* 139
Blakeney, *St Nicholas* 83
Burnham Overy, *St Clement* 27
Castle Rising, *St Lawrence* 37
Diss, *St Mary the Virgin* 96
East Barsham, *All Saints* 196
East Harling, *St Peter & St Paul* 97
East Lexham, *St Andrew* 68
Flitcham, *St Mary the Virgin* 192
Garboldisham, *St John the Baptist* 164
Great Dunham, *St Andrew* 20
Great Massingham, *St Mary* 162
Great Walsingham, *St Peter* 190
Hargham, *All Saints* 202
Heacham, *St Mary the Virgin* 187
Hunstanton, *Old Hunstanton* 116
Holme-next-the-Sea, *St Mary the Virgin* 106
Ingworth, *St Lawrence* 196
Kettlestone, *All Saints* 65
King's Lynn, *King's Lynn Minster* 148
Little Walsingham, *St Mary & All Saints* 190
Mattishall Mattishall 96
Norwich, *St Peter Mancroft* 75

# INDEX

Norwich, *St Stephen* 108
Pulham, *St Mary* 167
Ranworth, *St Helen* 177
Shelton, *St Mary* 129
Snettisham, *St Mary* 83
South Lopham, *St Andrews* 25
Tilney cum Islington, *St Mary* 199
Trunch, *St Botolph* 179
Swaffham, *St Peter & St Paul* 97
Syderstone, *St Mary* 69
Warham, *All Saints* 179
Waterden, *All Saints* 203
West Walton, *St Mary* 165
Wheatacre, *All Saints* 82
Winterton-on-Sea, *Holy Trinity and All Saints* 82
Wymondham, *Wymondham Abbey* 194-5

## NORTHAMPTONSHIRE
Bix, *St James* 198
Boughton, *St John the Baptist* 197
Brixworth, *All Saints* 14
Earls Barton, *All Saints* 13
Fotheringhay, *St Mary & All Saints* 61
Great Oakley, *St Michael* 123
Holdenby, *All Saints* 135
Lowick, *St Peter* 61
Newnham, *St Michael & All Angels* 74
Northampton, *The Church Of The Holy Sepulchre* 61
Northampton, *St Peter* 35
Syresham, *St James* 166
Wilby, *St Mary* 63

## NORTHUMBERLAND
Ancroft, *St Anne* 86
Bywell, *St Andrew* 13

## OXFORDSHIRE
Abingdon, *St Helen* 104
Bicester, *St Edburg* 104
Bloxham, *St Mary* 63
Burford, *St John* 170
Cassington, *St Peter* 22
Castleton, *St Edmund* 110
Chipping Norton, *St Mary the Virgin* 127
Checkendon, *St Peter & St Paul* 43
Cuddesdon, *All Saints* 155
Ewelme, *St Mary* 130
Hook Norton, *St Peter* 137
Iffley, *St Mary the Virgin* 22
Marsh Baldon, *St Peter* 185
Newnham Murren, *St Mary* 123
Oxford, *St Michael* 15
Oxford, *University Church* 110
South Newington, *St Peter ad Vincula* 167
Stanton St John, *St John* 137
Uffington, *St Mary* 60

## RUTLAND
Lyddington, *St Andrew* 81

## SOMERSET
Barton St David, Glastonbury, *St David* 64
Bath, *Bath Abbey* 151
Bristol, *All Saints Corn St* 107
Bristol, *St John in the Gate* 142
Clevedon, *St Andrew* 28
Crowcombe, *Church of the Holy Ghost* 132
Doulting, *St Aldhelm* 62
Exton, *St Peter* 108
Frome, *St John the Baptist* 143
Ilminster, *St Mary* 67
Laverton, *St Mary* 178
Meare, *St Mary* 55
North Perrot, *St Martin* 160
Pilton, *St John the Baptist* 132
Taunton, *St James* 67
Tintinhull, *St Margaret* 55
Weston Super Mare, *Old St Nicholas Uphill* 193

## SUFFOLK

Aldeburgh, *St Peter & St Paul* 124
Bawdsey, *St Mary the Virgin* 176
Blythburgh, *Holy Trinity* 127
Boxford, *St Mary* 97
Bungay, *St Mary* 69
Cavendish, *St Mary the Virgin* 54
Clare, *St Peter & St Paul* 74
Coddenham, *St Mary* 166
Corton, *St Bartholomew* 201
Covehithe, *St Andrews* 182
Dallinghoo, *St Mary* 192
Denton, *St Mary* 129
Earl Stonham, *St Mary* 53
East Bergholt, *St Mary* 183
Little Cornard, *All Saints* 97
Long Melford, *Holy Trinity* 125
Mutford, *St Andrew* 70
Nayland, *St James* 165
Needham Market, *St John the Baptist* 111
Pakefield, *All Saints & St Margaret* 141
Stanton, *St John the Baptist* 197
Stoke-by-Nayland, *St Mary the Virgin* 50
Southwold, *St Edmund* 164
Thorington, *St Peter* 71
Wickham Market, *All Saints* 60
Wissington, *St Mary* 43
Wortham, *St Mary the Virgin* 70

## EAST SUSSEX

Berwick, *St Michael & All Angels* 120
Hamsey, Offham, Lewes, *St Peter* 175
Icklesham, *All Saints & St Nicolas* 73
Newhaven, *St Michael* 11
Piddinghoe, Lewes, *St John* 140
Southease, *St Peter* 68
Ticehurst, *St Mary* 180

## WEST SUSSEX

Billingshurst, *St Mary* 87
Bosham, *Holy Trinity* 8
Botolphs, *St Botolph's* 174
Broadwater, *St Mary* 161
Climping, *St Mary* 122
Shipley, *St Mary the Virgin* 21
Sompting, *St Mary* 18
Steyning, *St Andrew & St Cuthman* 133
Tillington, *All Hallows* 95

## WILTSHIRE

Amesbury, *St Mary* 30
Bradford on Avon, *St Laurence* 19
Calne, *St Mary* 116
Corsham, *St Bartholomew* 117
Devizes, *St John the Baptist* 76
Edington, *Edington Priory Church* 55
Great Chalfield, *All Saints* 117
Inglesham, *St John the Baptist* 99
Kilmington, *St Mary* 134
Lacock, *St Cyriac* 157
Malmesbury, *Malmesbury Abbey* 188
Melksham, *St Michael & All Angels* 105
Purton, *St Mary* 103
Salisbury, *St Thomas's* 107
Stapleford, *St Mary* 109
Warminster, *St Denys* 130

## YORKSHIRE

Beverley, *St Mary* 64
Birkin, Ferrybridge 45
Campsall, *St Mary Magdalene* 150
Cawood, *All Saints* 113
Coxwold, *St Michael* 62
Filey, *St Oswald* 29
Halifax, *St Mary* 124
Hemingborough, *St Mary* 78
Kingston on Hull, *Hull Minster* 126
Kirby Underdale, *All Saints* 138
Lastingham, *St Mary* 46
Old Malton, *St Mary's Priory* 185
Pontefract, *All Saints* 59
Roos, *All Saints* 154
Scarborough, *St Mary* 192
Tickhill, *St Mary* 56
Wawne, *St Peter* 114